Published by Evans Brothers Limited
2A Portman Mansions
Chiltern Street
London W1U 6NR

© Evans Brothers Limited 2006

First published 2006

Printed in China by WKT Co., Ltd

British Library Cataloguing in Publication data.

Powell, Jillian
Charlotte has Impaired Vision. - (Like Me, Like You)
1. Children with visual disabilities - Juvenile literature
2. Vision disorders - Juvenile literature
I. Title
364. 4'1

ISBN 0237530325
13-digit ISBN (from 1 January 2007) 978 0 237 53032 7

Acknowledgements

The author and publisher would like to thank the following
for their help with this book:

Charlotte Coulton and family, the staff of Collingtree
Primary School, Daisy Utting and Sophie Langer.

At RNIB: Sue Wright, Karen Porter and Mary McDonald

All photographs by Gareth Boden

Credits

Editor: Julia Bird
Designer: Mark Holt
Production: Jenny Mulvanny

VISIT OUR WEBSITE
Evans
www.evansbooks.co.uk

RNIB

Reg charity 226227

LIKE ME LIKE YOU

Charlotte has IMPAIRED VISION

JILLIAN POWELL

Evans

Hi, my name is Charlotte. I live at home with Mum and Dad, my brother Reece and my baby sister Sasha. I like swimming, playing on the trampoline and tap dancing.

SIGHT PROBLEMS

Some people are born with a visual impairment. Others have sight problems later on and a few lose their sight because of an accident.

I have **impaired vision**. It means I can't see as well as most people.

I can't see anything with my right eye and I can only see poorly with my left eye. I need extra help to get around safely and to do things like reading.

When I'm at home, I use the feel of things to help me get around safely. I have to take extra care on the stairs. Mum makes sure there is nothing on the floor that could trip me up, which isn't easy with Reece around!

It's fun helping Mum bath my baby sister Sasha. Sasha likes it when I sing to her.

I use a **short cane** to help me get around when I go out. It helps me check where things are as I go along. At the moment, I need someone to help me get across the road safely. When I'm older, I'll use a **long cane** so I can cross the road by myself.

When I cross the road, my cane warns drivers that I can't see them very well.

At school, I have a sloping board so I can see my work better when I am reading or writing. A learning support assistant helps me when I need it in class. She copies all my work into **big print** so I can see it more easily.

12

Art is one of my favourite lessons. Today I'm using glue sticks in bright colours to stick things on to a collage I'm making.

12 IN 1000

Around 12 in 1000 children worldwide have impaired vision

When I use a computer, I look at big print on a yellow screen, which is easier for me to see. My computer has a big toolbar and cursor and there are **bumpons** on the keys to help me find them.

Sometimes I need a bit of help from my learning support assistant when I have a lot of reading to do. My eyes can get tired looking at computers, so I don't spend much time playing on them.

When I'm looking at diagrams, pictures or maps, I use my **CCTV**. I can put my books on to it and it makes everything look bigger on the screen so I can see it more easily.

I have other things to help me in class, like my **talking calculator** and a ruler that helps me measure things by touch. In science today, I'm using a special jug to measure out some water.

17

My learning support assistant is helping me to learn **braille**. I have learned the braille alphabet, and now I'm learning to read whole words and sentences.

I'm also learning how to type in braille. I use a **brailler** which has six keys. They type raised dots that spell out letters and words.

BRAILLE

Braille uses raised dots that can be read by touch to spell out letters, numbers and words. Only a small number of children with a visual impairment use braille; most use large print instead.

After school, my friend Daisy comes over to play with my dolls' house. The furniture and the dolls are very small so it's easier for me to see them whole. Big things are harder for me to see because I can only see part of them.

20

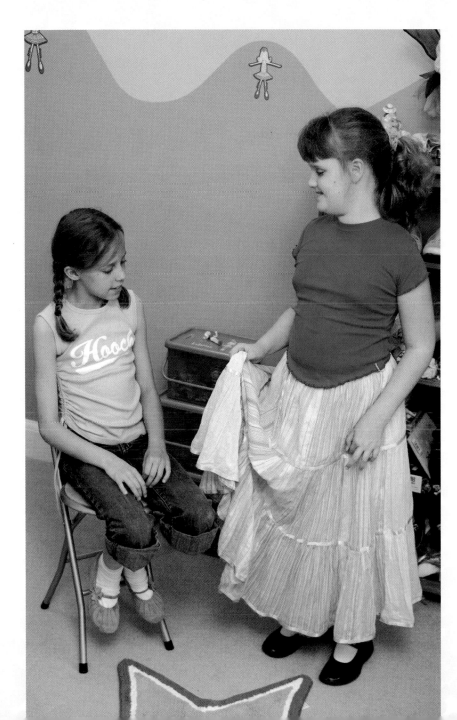

I show Daisy a skirt I got when I went shopping with Mum. I like choosing my own clothes. I pick the colours I like, but sometimes Mum has to help me find the right sizes, because I can't see them clearly.

My **talking watch** tells me it's time for my tap class. Daisy and I go to a tap class at our gym once a week. Sometimes we practise at home. Mum puts down boards for us to try out our steps. I love the sound of our tap shoes!

When we're in class, I stand near the teacher so I can see her better. Sometimes she comes over to make sure I can follow the steps properly.

When I get home, Mum is on the telephone to the hospital about my check-up tomorrow. I have to go for a check-up three times a year. The doctors check that my sight is not getting any worse. I do a sight test and they shine a light in my eyes to see if there are any changes.

Then I sit down to watch television. I have my own chair so I can sit close enough to see the screen. I like cartoons best!

Being visually impaired means that some things can be harder for me, like using mobile phones or computers.

I can play with my tamagotchi, but I have to hold it very close to my face to see it properly.

But I can still enjoy my favourite things like tap dancing, watching television and playing on the swings with my brother Reece!

Glossary

Big print writing in large letters, used in books or on computer screens

Braille a system for reading and writing in raised dots, invented by Louis Braille (1809-52) in 1829

Brailler a machine that prints braille

Bumpons raised dots on computer keys

CCTV closed circuit television, which shows enlarged images on a screen

Impaired vision when someone has problems with their sight that cannot be corrected by glasses or surgery

Long cane/short cane white canes used by blind or visually impaired people to help them get around safely

Talking calculator a calculator that says everything that is entered aloud

Talking watch a watch that tells the time aloud

Index

Further Information

UNITED KINGDOM
Royal National Institute of the Blind
Tel: 020 7388 1266
www.rnib.org.uk
RNIB is the UK's leading charity helping people
with sight problems. Call RNIB's helpline on
0845 766 9999 for information, support and
advice for anyone with a sight problem and their
families.

National Blind Children's Society
Tel: 01278 764 764
www.nbcs.org.uk
Support and information for blind and partially
sighted children and their carers. Offers grants
and helps fund leisure activities and holidays for
blind and partially sighted children.

UNITED STATES OF AMERICA
American Foundation for the Blind
Tel: (212) 502 7600
www.afb.org
Information and facts, with a special section on
Braille and a 'Braille bug' club for children.

AUSTRALIA
Royal Society for the Blind
Tel: (08) 8232 4777
www.rsb.org.au
Support and services for blind and visually
impaired people, with lots of links to other
websites and special children's section.

NEW ZEALAND
Royal New Zealand Foundation for the Blind
Tel: 0800 24 33 33
www.rnzfb.org.nz
Charity for blind and partially sighted people and
their families with links to children's websites.

BOOKS
Meet Georgia who is Blind, Dianne Church,
Franklin Watts 2003

My Friend is Blind, N. Edwards,
Belitha 2004

When It's Hard to See, J. Condon,
Franklin Watts 2002

29